Flowers
of the
Wayside

Elisabeth Trotignon

Illustrations
Claire Felloni
Frédérique Schwebel
and
Dominique Mansion
Fernand Mognetti

Translated by
Josephine Weightman

HarperCollins*Publishers*

COLLINS WATCH GUIDES

Illustrations: Frédéric Denhez
Black and white artwork: François
Desbordes
Translation: Josephine Weightman

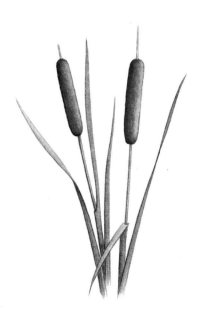

ISBN 0 00 220092 9
© Éditions Gallimard, Paris, 1996
© in this English translation HarperCollins*Publishers*, London, 1997
Printed and bound in Italy

Contents

The Countryside

The countryside of Western Europe enjoys a mild, moist climate and there are large expanses of lowland. Wild flowers grow almost everywhere: in meadows or arable fields, woodland or heathland, in and around pond edges and even on the outskirts of villages. So you don't have to go a long way to take your first steps in studying flowers! Moreover, very often roadside verges have enough to interest a beginner.

● The most insignificant places may harbour a large number of plants: take for example this **field** which is covered in buttercups in May before being cut for hay or grazed by cattle. While these flowers are easy to see, there are many others, less striking, which you can find if you look carefully.

Gently rolling landscape with hedges and trees, often associated with a moist climate

Hedge with broad-leaved trees and shrubs: shade-loving plants grow at its foot

Cattle-grazed meadow: mostly perennial plants grow here

● The flower covering almost all this **meadow** is cuckooflower. It prefers a light situation on cool rather damp clay soils. You would be very unlikely to see it near a poppy or cornflower.

● Poppies and cornflowers are arable weeds, that is to say they grow in **cultivated fields**. Many species have a particular ecological niche. In the picture above, the presence of so many flowers indicates that the field has not been treated with chemicals.

● This **traditional landscape** is very rich botanically because it offers several habitats: warm, well-lit open areas (the meadows) and shady edges (trees and hedges) where meadow species and woodland species, such as the wood anemone, occur together.

● The flora of an area is determined by the nature of the soil and the local climate, but also by the the action of man, animals and plants. This **heathland** is mainly found in regions where rainfall is quite high, the soils are acid and formerly heavily grazed.

Sun-loving plants preferring richer soils are abundant on waysides

Footpath Profile

Footpaths are often very rich botanically: their edges are not 'improved' as, unlike meadows and cornfields, they receive no fertiliser or herbicide. They shelter numerous species not found elsewhere as a result of agricultural or industrial practices. Dry and damp habitats often occur side by side, on banks or ditches or on deep or shallow soils, in a space of a few square metres.

● Formally, in very stony areas, people used to use the rocks to build low walls. Stone walls are not lacking in flowers. The plants must, however, be those adapted for rather tough conditions such as shortage of water and very shallow soils.

Bank

Ditch

● Ditches are often water-filled: rushes grow quickly and may become invasive and contribute to the silting-up process.

● Grassy wayside edges contain more colourful flowering plants when the soil is shallow and lacks nutrients. Where the soil is deep and rich, grasses are dominant and impede the growth of other plants.

● Verges beside **minor roads** may provide a pleasant surprise especially in spring.

● **Straight tracks** occur only in areas of intensive agriculture. Their verges are the only remaining refuge for wildlife.

● **Sunken lanes** are very ancient. Often enclosed, damp and shady, they support a special range of plants which does not occur in drier, more exposed places.

● **Woodland path edges** support plants adapted to two major constraints, shade and humidity. Bluebells, for example, occur in vast blue sheets in broad-leaved woodland.

● Paths in many areas present the same profile. The access path itself is bordered by a wide verge supporting herbaceous plants then by a ditch which carries away rain water.

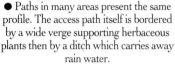

Path

Rut created by the wheels of vehicles. It fills up with water after rain.

● Generally, the path is used by agricultural machinery and walkers. However, if it is not maintained, it is quickly invaded by vegetation and soon becomes impassable.

Picture Guide

Botanising is very simple: almost all year long, a succession of plants can be seen in flower beside paths. But the same plants cannot be seen everywhere. Each species has its preferred habitat with a particular kind of soil, aspect and moisture content. Nearly every plant, even the most humble, acts as an indicator for the habitat in which it grows. However, there are some undemanding plants which occur anywhere.

● The family to which the plant belongs is given in brackets.

Dandelion (Asteraceae)

Daisy (Asteraceae)

Shepherd's purse (Brassicaceae)

Red dead nettle (Lamiaceae)

Sweet violet (Violaceae)

Cowslip (Primulaceae)

Greater stitchwort (Caryophyllaceae)

Meadow buttercup (Ranunculaceae)

Solomon's seal (Liliaceae)

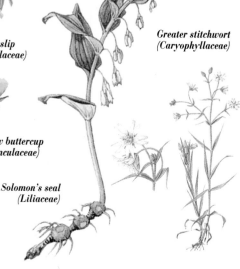

to Plants in this Book

Wood anemone
(Ranunculaceae)

Good King Henry
(Chenopodiaceae)

Germander speedwell
(Scrophulariaceae)

Salad burnet
(Rosaceae)

Yellow iris
(Iridaceae)

Scentless mayweed
(Asteraceae)

Cuckooflower
(Brassicaceae)

Mugwort *(Asteraceae)*

Bird's-foot trefoil
(Fabaceae)

Scarlet pimpernel
(Primulaceae)

Cornflower
(Asteraceae)

Bell heather
(Ericaceae)

Purple loosestrife
(Lythraceae)

Cock's-foot
(Poaceae)

Land under Cultivation

Weeds – unwanted plants – often persist on arable land. Nowadays they are disappearing because they cannot tolerate fertilisers and insecticides or, on the other hand, are proliferating because they are resistant to such products. However they all survive beside paths where wildlife is still fairly well protected.

● **Scentless mayweed** blooms from June to October.

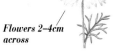

Flowers 2–4cm across

● **Common fumitory** is frequent on chalky and clay soils.

Flowers in clusters

Deeply cut leaves

Petals fused together like a funnel

● The flowers of the **field bindweed** do not open in dull weather. The stems twine around other plants in an anticlockwise direction.

Pink flowers

Reddish stem

Toothed leaves

Alternate leaves with large basal lobes

● **Red dead nettle** is unpopular with gardeners as it grows everywhere and has an unpleasant smell.

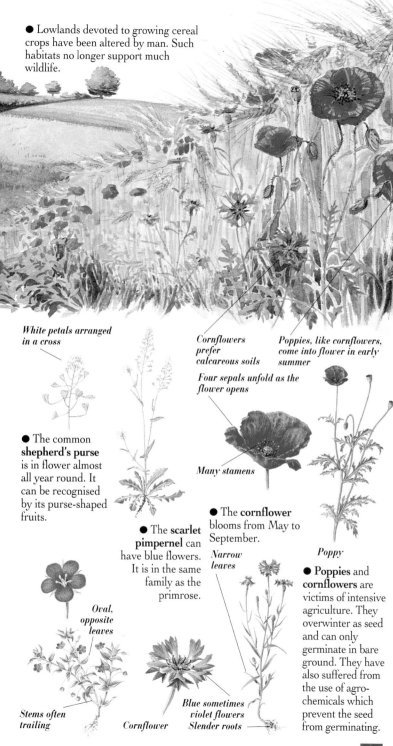

● Lowlands devoted to growing cereal crops have been altered by man. Such habitats no longer support much wildlife.

White petals arranged in a cross

● The common **shepherd's purse** is in flower almost all year round. It can be recognised by its purse-shaped fruits.

Cornflowers prefer calcareous soils

Poppies, like cornflowers, come into flower in early summer

Four sepals unfold as the flower opens

Many stamens

● The **scarlet pimpernel** can have blue flowers. It is in the same family as the primrose.

● The **cornflower** blooms from May to September.

Narrow leaves

Poppy

Oval, opposite leaves

Stems often trailing

Cornflower

Blue sometimes violet flowers

Slender roots

● **Poppies** and **cornflowers** are victims of intensive agriculture. They overwinter as seed and can only germinate in bare ground. They have also suffered from the use of agro-chemicals which prevent the seed from germinating.

Wide three-lobed lip

Pale red lip with dark spots

Military orchid

Simple alternate leaves

Small flowers

Globularia

Lip shape imitates a fly

White to dark crimson

Blue-violet flowers massed into a head

Green-winged orchid

Fly orchid

● In Europe, **orchids** (Orchidaceae) are not as striking as in hot tropical areas. Nevertheless their delicate flowers attract insects which come and pollinate them.

● Most orchids that occur on chalky grassland flower in June and July.

● **Globularia** grows well on rocky, sun-warmed slopes.

● Chalky grasslands are often found on sunny slopes. As they are not cultivated, they can be spotted from some distance away, adding to the diversity of the countryside.

Chalky Grassland

On chalky grassland the soil is shallow and poor in nutrients and water but, on the other hand, it warms up quickly. Vegetation here is rich and diverse: it comprises low perennial plants adapted to heat and dry conditions, often southern in origin. Several rare orchids grow on these lime-rich soils.

● Chalky grassland has often been woodland in former days and has been cleared and grazed by sheep. Nowadays, many areas are unmanaged.

Pink flowers arranged in a false umbel

Opposite leaves

● **Marjoram** is very aromatic.

● Perennial herbaceous plants dominate chalky grassland. Their vegetative system (roots, bulbs and tubers) spreads out, preventing other plants from growing.

Mignonette

● **Mignonette** likes dry open and preferably stony situations. It flowers in early summer.

● **Upright brome** is a perennial grass with flat leaves.

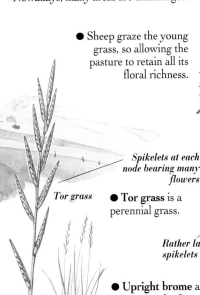

● Sheep graze the young grass, so allowing the pasture to retain all its floral richness.

Spikelets at each node bearing many flowers

Tor grass

● **Tor grass** is a perennial grass.

Rather large spikelets

Upright brome

● **Upright brome** and **tor grass** are among the first plants to colonise abandoned chalky grassland. Their root system enables them to increase rapidly so they tend to develop at the expense of other species.

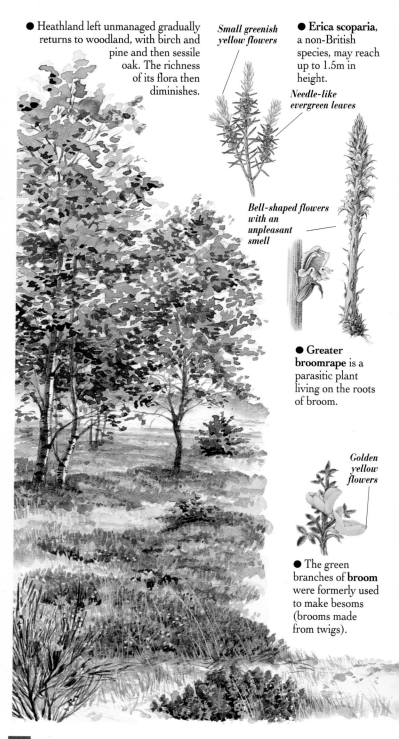

● Heathland left unmanaged gradually returns to woodland, with birch and pine and then sessile oak. The richness of its flora then diminishes.

Small greenish yellow flowers

● **Erica scoparia**, a non-British species, may reach up to 1.5m in height.

Needle-like evergreen leaves

Bell-shaped flowers with an unpleasant smell

● **Greater broomrape** is a parasitic plant living on the roots of broom.

Golden yellow flowers

● The green branches of **broom** were formerly used to make besoms (brooms made from twigs).

Acid Heathland

Regular pink flowers

Large pink sepals

Little purple bells with toothed margins

Elongated clusters

● **Heather** is an evergreen shrublet less than one metre tall. It prefers warm situations and is often found growing with bell heather.

Red-brown erect stems

● **Bell heather** should not be confused with heather as it blooms earlier (June–August, instead of July–September).

Pale blue flowers in a spike

Flowers arising from the leaf axils

Heath speedwell

● **Heath speedwell** usually grows on dry acid soils in association with bell heather.

Heathlands are characteristically dominated by low woody shrubs with small thick leaves; they developed from former woodland which was cleared and then grazed by small livestock. Nowadays they are being used for arable farming but the poor, impoverished acid soils, in which plant remains are very slow to decompose, will never yield good crops.

Flowers in dense clusters

White asphodel

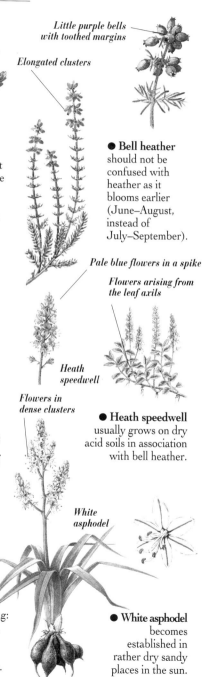

● Heathlands are particularly interesting: scenically, on account of the yellow and purple flowers of the shrubs; and botanically because of the rare and endangered species hidden among them.

● **White asphodel** becomes established in rather dry sandy places in the sun.

15

Meadows on Dry Soils

Yellow flowers often flushed with orange

3–6 flowers in a head

● **Bird's-foot trefoil** may have an extensive root system in dry situations.

White sometimes pinkish flowers arranged in a flat head

Yarrow

● **Yarrow,** a slightly aromatic plant, is very resistant to drought.

Farmers sow fodder plants in meadows (for example, grasses and leguminous plants) for hay or as pasture for stock. Among them, especially before the spring cut, appear beautiful, often brightly coloured, perennial plants

Greenish flowers with some red

Toothed leaflets

Long sepal

Dark violet blue flower

● Some campanulas carry their flowers in dense clusters.

● **Salad burnet** has heads of modest flowers lacking petals; the lower flowers are male, the middle ones are hermaphrodite, and the upper female.

● The **campanulas** or bellflowers, such as the **harebell** are common in meadows. Their large blue bell-shaped flowers resemble gentians but differ by having alternate not opposite leaves.

Rosette of leaves at the base

Harebell

● Grasses are mostly perennial plants and have long narrow leaves. Pollen from their flower spikes is transported by the wind. Take care! It may bring on an attack of hay fever.

● In closely grazed and fenced meadows, the plants you see are mainly those species (too tough, spiny or poisonous) which stock cannot eat.

● The **ox-eye daisy** covers large areas forming splendid white patches against the green grass.

Oval leaves

Numerous often trailing stems

● **Chickweed** flowers all year round.

Flowers start green then turn yellow

● **Cock's-foot** is sown for hay. To help it grow, the farmer puts nitrogenous fertiliser on the meadow.

●The pleasant smell of **sweet vernal grass** can be detected in dry weather.

Damp Meadows

Flowers in a head

Yellow flowers entirely of ray florets

Roots of young plants can be eaten

● **Viper's-grass** grows in very wet meadows.

Damp meadows are generally of lower agricultural value than dry meadows because of the wetness and poor soil. But they are very interesting botanically as they support many species. They still need to be maintained regularly by cutting or grazing.

The grasses in the marshy bottom of the meadow are more rank and greener

White, slightly pinkish flowers with violet veins

Upright ribbed stem

● **Field horsetail** is a flowerless plant. It scatters spores from its brown cones. Slender green stems appear later.

Fruits: narrow capsules

Leaves forming sheaths at the nodes

● **Cuckooflower** is one of the first flowers to appear in the damp meadow bottom.

● Damp meadows, which do not make any money for the farmer, are under threat today. Farmers seek to replace them either with poplar plantations, or by improving drainage and applying fertiliser. More and more often they are left unmanaged.

and Valley Bottoms

Five petals divided into four narrow lobes

Three-lobed lip

● **Meadowsweet** grows in really damp places. It blooms from June to September.

● **Loose-flowered orchid** occurs in marshy and rather sandy sites.

● **Ragged robin** flowers in May.

Reddish stem

Underside of the leaves white and downy

Marsh bedstraw

Compact rush

Meadow buttercup

Ragged robin

Yorkshire fog

Loose-flowered orchid

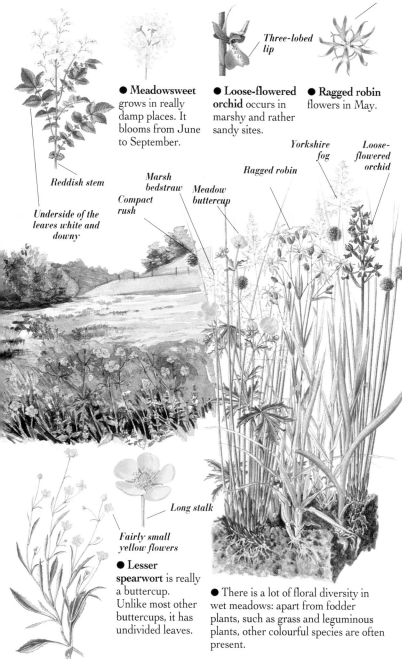

Long stalk

Fairly small yellow flowers

● **Lesser spearwort** is really a buttercup. Unlike most other buttercups, it has undivided leaves.

● There is a lot of floral diversity in wet meadows: apart from fodder plants, such as grass and leguminous plants, other colourful species are often present.

Pond Edges

Ponds present great floral diversity: on the bank where it is dry, plants common to other habitats grow; on the other hand, where soil comes in contact with water, plants grow which are able to tolerate very wet conditions in the winter and drought conditions in the summer.

Reddish purple flowers in a terminal spike

● **Yellow iris** grows in clumps at the water's edge where the wet soil is high in nutrients. It flowers in June.

Opposite leaves

● **Purple loosestrife**, like the iris, favours damp soils.

Sword-like leaves

Cylindrical stalk

Fleshy, creeping rhizome

No scent

● A pond is an expanse of shallow water, often man-made, in a natural depression. It has an impermeable clay bottom.

Common reed forms large stands

Rush

Yellow iris

● Each bulrush head produces about 250,000 seeds.

Female flowers *Male flowers*

● When abundant, **reed canary grass** shows that the habitat is becoming degraded.

Brownish flowers in a cluster

Bract

Inflorescence often purplish

Leaves with sharp edges

Long flat leaves

● **Bulrush** occurs on the banks of pools and artificial lakes. It tolerates summer drought well.

● Reeds are tall water-loving plants (up to 3m), growing stems which persist although dried out until the following spring. Common reed, reed canary grass and bulrush are the best known.

● **Soft rush** prefers the water-logged soil of the meadow adjoining the pool.

Lilac flowers on a terminal cluster

● **Common reed** is a perennial plant capable of growing to 5m high. Its rhizome is very long (up to several metres). It can tolerate both an excess or an absence of water.

● **Water mint** has a strong smell.

Bulrush

Golden yellow flowers

● All pond plants require sunlight. They take root in soils which are periodically water-soaked.

● **Yellow loosestrife** blooms from June to August on damp pond edges.

Large opposite leaves

Transport Lines

The borders of minor roads, railway lines and waterways support a wide range of plants that can withstand often dry and disturbed conditions. Many of them are alien species, whose seeds have arrived in produce of various kinds, having fallen from vehicles. Seeds are also scattered by cars and carried on people's shoes.

● Many plants, such as Chinese mugwort, rare at the beginning of the century, are very common today on railway embankments. This plant was brought back from China by the Verlot brothers in the mid-19th century.

Kestrel

The buddleia or butterfly bush also originates from China

Smooth blue-green linear leaves

Yellow flowers grouped into numerous small clusters

● **Golden rod** comes from North America. It is a common garden plant and is often seen in the wild near houses.

Clusters of bright yellow to orange flowers

● **Common toadflax** looks rather like the garden snapdragon. It flowers from May to September in sunny situations.

Slightly toothed leaves

Velvety stem

Goldfinch

● Along canals the flora may be dominated by species introduced by boats.

Pale yellow tubular flowers, grouped into small heads

● Plants in the umbellifer family (carrot and cow parsley) are easily recognised because the flowers are borne in umbels and the leaves give off a strong smell when crushed.

● **Cow parsley** prefers damp but sunny places, rich in nitrogen.

Narrow lanceolate leaves

Umbel with 3-7 rays

Shiny leaves

● **Canadian fleabane** was introduced into Europe in the middle of the 19th century. It occurs on light soils, blooming from July to October. Its fruits are achenes.

Hollow deeply channelled stem

23

Wasteland

Climate and the nature of the soil cannot alone account for the presence of some plants on wasteland. Very often, in fact, wastelands have been trampled, become hard-packed and, as a result, are liable to flooding; a specialised flora becomes established, dominated by annual plants which form patches here and there, covering the ground.

Tubular yellow flowers

Leaves velvety beneath

● **Mugwort** is a clump-forming perennial plant with a woody stock. It flowers from July to September.

● **White dead nettle** looks like a stinging nettle but does not sting.

● The **daisy** is a perennial which flowers almost all through the year. But it is best seen in spring when vegetation is still low.

Leaves in a rosette

White ray florets

Yellow tubular florets

Ray florets close up in rainy weather

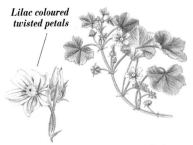

Lilac coloured twisted petals

● **Dwarf mallow** is an annual plant with many branching stems. The flower closes at night and in bad weather.

● **Dandelions** grow in sunny spots.

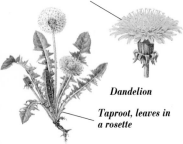

Dandelion

Taproot, leaves in a rosette

● Dandelions and daisies occur everywhere, in towns as well as in the countryside. They are easily recognised.

Yellow-green flowers

Greater plantain

Flowers densely packed in a long greenish spike

Green flowers in terminal clusters

Good King Henry

● **Good King Henry** used to be commonly eaten as a vegetable. It still occurs frequently near farms.

Dark green spear-shaped leaves

● **Greater plantain** favours hard-packed ground in sunny places. In towns it can often be found on regularly mown lawns.

Wide oval leaves with very prominent veins

● Plants in wasteland are often tall and stiffly erect. They flower during the summer but remain standing all winter when their dried fruits can be seen.

Sunken Lanes

Sunken lanes follow the lie of the land. Formerly they were kept open by the repeated passage of farm animals. Nowadays they are falling more and more into disuse as they are unsuitable for modern farm machinery. However they are very pleasant places for walks.

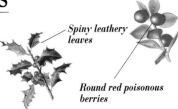

Spiny leathery leaves

Round red poisonous berries

● **Holly** is a small evergreen tree; only the females bear berries in autumn.

● **Butcher's broom** is a small evergreen shrub. The apparent leaves are actually flattened stems. The true leaves are reduced to scales.

● In sunken lanes the shade and humidity created by overhanging trees, produce very special conditions for the growth of certain plants.

Bell-shaped flowers with lobes

● **Navelwort** is a small fleshy plant which characteristically grows on banks which began as vertical-sided stone walls. It often occurs with common polypody.

Fleshy leaves with a central navel-like depression

Round sori (masses of sporangia)

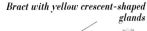

Bract with yellow crescent-shaped glands

● **Wood spurge** has no petals or sepals but yellowish green inflorescences arranged in an umbel. Each consists of a female flower surrounded by several male flowers.

Reddish brown stem, naked below

● **Common polypody** is a fern with a thick rhizome bearing russet scales.

Lanceolate fronds with 10–25 pairs of lobes

Five violet-blue petals with cut-off tips

Triangular frond

● The **periwinkle** is in flower from spring to autumn but its shiny leaves persist all winter.

● All violets look alike and tend to hybridise: they are difficult to tell apart.

Heart-shaped toothed leaves

The young frond is rolled up like a crozier

● **Bracken** is a common perennial fern which is difficult to eradicate. It thrives on acid soils in half-shade. The dry fronds stand all winter.

Bracken may reach a height of 2m

● The **common dog violet** has no scent. It blooms in April on fairly dry, acid soils.

Rather large bluish flowers

Old Walls in Towns

On and at the foot of old walls grow specialised plants, dominated by species requiring soil high in nitrogen and therefore the proximity of man. Some manage to take hold in the smallest crack – you may well wonder how they succeed in growing!

Wall rue is a small fern that grows well on sunny walls and calcareous rocks

Ivy-leaved toadflax has lilac flowers with a yellow throat

● **Greater celandine** grows in the shade all summer long. It prefers rather cool soils.

● **Pellitory of the wall** thrives in cracks in calcareous walls. It belongs to the same family as the stinging nettle but does not sting.

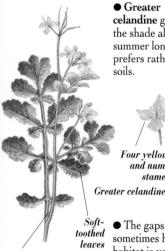

Four yellow petals and numerous stamens

Greater celandine

Acuminate leaves 5cm long

Flowers in small clusters

Soft-toothed leaves

Velvety stalk

● The gaps beneath drain covers sometimes harbour plants. This novel habitat is usually short-lived.

Reddish branching stem

Young tree of heaven

Small purple flowers of ivy-leaved toadflax

The leaf litter is gradually turned into humus by the action of bacteria and fungi

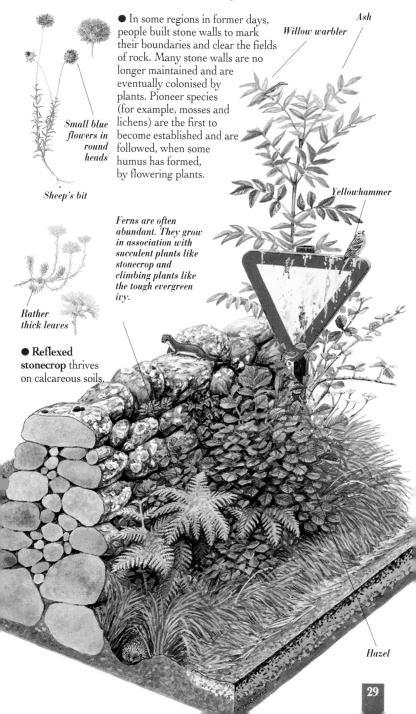

Small blue flowers in round heads

Sheep's bit

● In some regions in former days, people built stone walls to mark their boundaries and clear the fields of rock. Many stone walls are no longer maintained and are eventually colonised by plants. Pioneer species (for example, mosses and lichens) are the first to become established and are followed, when some humus has formed, by flowering plants.

Ash

Willow warbler

Yellowhammer

Ferns are often abundant. They grow in association with succulent plants like stonecrop and climbing plants like the tough evergreen ivy.

Rather thick leaves

● **Reflexed stonecrop** thrives on calcareous soils.

Hazel

29

Hedges

Hedges are a habitat created and exploited by man: in some areas, patches of land were enclosed with living fences – hedges – for a range of uses. They were boundaries to property, shelter for stock and a source of timber all in one. These hedges were composed of trees, shrubs and low-growing plants which were adapted to local conditions.

Dark purple flowers with five petals

Rosette of heart-shaped leaves with crenate edges

● **Sweet violet** has a thick stock which sends out stolons. The flowers are heavily scented.

● Nowadays man tends to trim the hedge or remove it entirely especially when several fields are made into one. In so doing he alters the balance of nature.

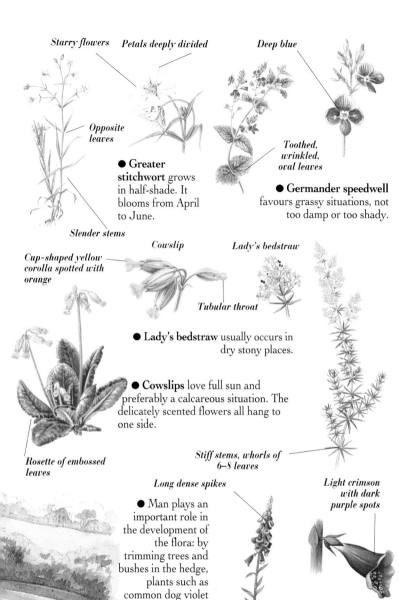

Starry flowers

Petals deeply divided

Deep blue

Opposite leaves

● **Greater stitchwort** grows in half-shade. It blooms from April to June.

Toothed, wrinkled, oval leaves

● **Germander speedwell** favours grassy situations, not too damp or too shady.

Slender stems

Cowslip

Lady's bedstraw

Cup-shaped yellow corolla spotted with orange

Tubular throat

● **Lady's bedstraw** usually occurs in dry stony places.

● **Cowslips** love full sun and preferably a calcareous situation. The delicately scented flowers all hang to one side.

Rosette of embossed leaves

Stiff stems, whorls of 6–8 leaves

Long dense spikes

● Man plays an important role in the development of the flora: by trimming trees and bushes in the hedge, plants such as common dog violet and yarrow are encouraged to grow. On the other hand, if he stops cutting, shade increases at the foot of the hedge and these same species become straggly and die out.

Light crimson with dark purple spots

● **Foxgloves** cannot be missed. They need a sunny spot on acid soils and flower briefly in June.

31

Woodland Floo

There are many flowers in spring in broad-leaved woodland (oak, hornbeam, beech): the trees have not yet got their leaves so the light essential for growth filters through. Early in the year the woodland floor is covered in colourful sheets of bluebells, ramsoms and lily of the valley.

Greenish white scentless bells hanging in clusters of 2–6

● **Solomon's seal**, in the lily family, flowers from April to June. This is a shade species preferring fairly cool soils.

Rhizome bearing scars from the stems of the previous year

Large pale green bract

Reddish purple club-shaped spadix

Leaves may be brown-spotted in spring

● **Lords and ladies** is a shade plant liking deep soils.

Starry six-petalled flower

Lanceolate leaves with parallel veins

● **Ramsoms** has a characteristic smell. It comes up in April in rather damp situations forming a carpet of white.

● The **bluebell** requires shade. It usually grows in moisture retentive soils.

Slender flowering stalk

Deeply cut leaves arise directly from the rhizome on stalks

White flowers lightly pink or violet flushed

Creeping rhizome

Pale yellow petals, with the lower lip streaked reddish brown

● The **wood anemone** or **windflower** opens in May in the shade under oak or beech.

● **Yellow archangel**, like the bluebell, flowers from April to June. It occurs in oak or beech forest.

Carpet of bluebells on the floor of broad-leaved woodland

Pine Woods

In Western Europe, coniferous woods are nearly always artificial as they have been planted for rapid timber production. They are often composed of a single species, which tends to impoverish the soil (by acidification), and light penetration is poor. Herbaceous plants are therefore fairly rare.

● **Creeping lady's tresses** flowers from July to September on dry acid soils where the humus is poorly decomposed. This mountain orchid is now becoming established in conifer plantations.

Small white flowers in a dense spike all facing the same way

Leaves with netted veins

Slender stems

Brownish flowers in a loose cluster

Bunches of scented flowers drooping in bud, erect later

Short fine stiff leaves

● **Yellow bird's-nest** is a parasitic plant which cannot produce chlorophyll. A fleshy plant with no green parts, it grows in the shade under conifers on rather dry soils. The scented flowers open in summer.

Leaves like scales

Numerous basal leaves

● **Silver hair-grass** grows fairly well on dry acid soils. As it requires light and warmth, it occurs in forest clearings.

Hairy wood-rush

● **Wild strawberry** grows on acid soils in full sun. With its numerous long stolons and noticeable red edible fruits it is easily found.

● **Hairy wood-rush** is a shade plant of fairly dry acid situations. The modest flowers open from March to May.

White flowers with five petals

Hairy stem

Basal leaves long-stalked with three oval leaflets

The 250,000 or so species of flowering plants are arranged in hundreds of different families, based primarily on the structure of the flowers. Leaves, stems and overall growth form vary greatly with the plants' habitats and are of little value in classification. But flowers are not greatly affected by the habitat and closely related species usually have very similar flowers, even if they live in very different places and have very different growth forms. The rose family, for example, contains plants ranging from apple trees, through strawberries and cinquefoils, but their flowers all have the same basic structure. The identification of plants therefore requires some idea of the various parts that go to make up a flower.

What is a Flower?

The flower has male (stamens) and female (carpels which enclose the ovules and fuse together to form the ovary) sexual organs. These organs are protected by two floral envelopes: the outer one (the calyx), is composed of sepals; the second, inner one (the corolla), is composed of petals.

Cuckooflower

Flower with four petals

The shape and arrangement of leaves on the stem varies from one species to the next. In this example, the leaf has six to twelve pairs of narrow lanceolate leaflets (the blade is very dissected).

Node

The leaves, using solar energy, are responsible for photosynthesis. They also enable the plant to respire and transpire.

The stem bears the flowers and leaves. The latter arise at the nodes. The stem may be long or short, hollow or solid, trailing or upright, smooth or hairy.

The stock has small roots which attach the plant to the ground and can travel far either outwards or downwards to extract the water and mineral salts needed by the plant

In this case, the stem is unbranched and hollow

Often attractive and highly coloured, the flower is the most conspicuous part of a plant and the one which immediately distinguishes it from others; above all, this is the part which protects the reproductive organs. The other parts, roots, stems and leaves, which differ from one species to the next, are just as indispensable to the function of the plant: the leaves carry out photosynthesis and respiration, the roots extract water and mineral salts from the soil and vessels in the stem transport the sap.

Tuberous root

Tufted roots

Adventitious roots

Rhizome   *Taproot*

Bulb

● **Roots** are of several different kinds, but not all underground parts are roots. The iris rhizome, the orchid tuber and the bluebell bulb are actually underground stems which store food. Roots can spring from stems above ground as well, and help to anchor them. These are called adventitious roots.

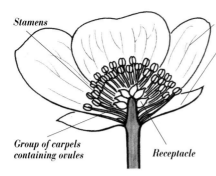

Stamens

Petals usually coloured

Sepals usually green

Group of carpels containing ovules

Receptacle

To reach the nectar, the insect cannot avoid brushing against the pollen-laden stamens

● **Fertilisation** occurs when the male element (pollen from the stamens) fuses with the female element (ovule) to form the seed. Cross fertilisation between flowers is desirable as this increases the vigour of the species.

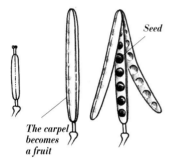

Seed

The carpel becomes a fruit

● The seed germinates in the ground. First the root emerges and buries itself in the soil. Then the stem of the embryo lengthens and the cotyledons develop into small leaves. Next new organs appear, the stems and leaves. The young plant can feed off food reserves in the cotyledons.

● **Pollination** occurs when the pollen from the stamens of one flower is transferred to the female part of another. It is often carried out by insects (for flowers which are highly coloured) or by wind (for those which are less so).

● After fertilisation, a carpel turns into a fruit. Fruits are very different from one species to another. They contain the seeds which, carried by the wind or by insects, reach the ground giving rise to new plants.

The stem grows taller then the first true leaves unfurl

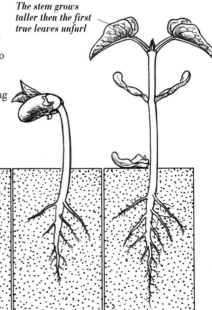

Monocotyledons

The 250,000 species of flowering plants that have been described fall into two classes: the monocotyledons and the dicotyledons. The monocotyledons are characterised by the presence of a single cotyledon (an embryonic leaf full of stored nutrient), long leaves with parallel veins and floral parts in threes. They include the grasses, orchids, lilies and several other families with world-wide distribution. Palm trees are also monocotyledons.

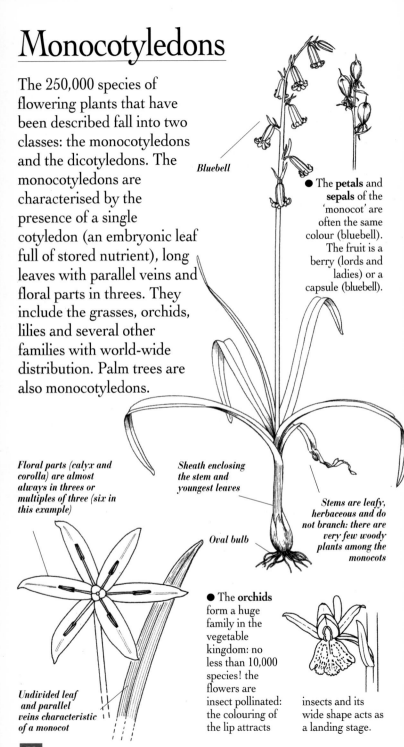

Bluebell

● The **petals** and **sepals** of the 'monocot' are often the same colour (bluebell). The fruit is a berry (lords and ladies) or a capsule (bluebell).

Floral parts (calyx and corolla) are almost always in threes or multiples of three (six in this example)

Sheath enclosing the stem and youngest leaves

Stems are leafy, herbaceous and do not branch: there are very few woody plants among the monocots

Oval bulb

Undivided leaf and parallel veins characteristic of a monocot

● The **orchids** form a huge family in the vegetable kingdom: no less than 10,000 species! the flowers are insect pollinated: the colouring of the lip attracts insects and its wide shape acts as a landing stage.

and Dicotyledons

The majority of flowering plants are placed with the dicotyledons. Herbaceous plants and trees ranging from a small chickweed to an oak are included here. The best known dicot families are the Apiaceae (carrot), Rosaceae, Fabaceae (peas) and Asteraceae (daisies). This class is characterised by the presence of two cotyledons, leaves with a network of veins and floral parts in multiples of four or five.

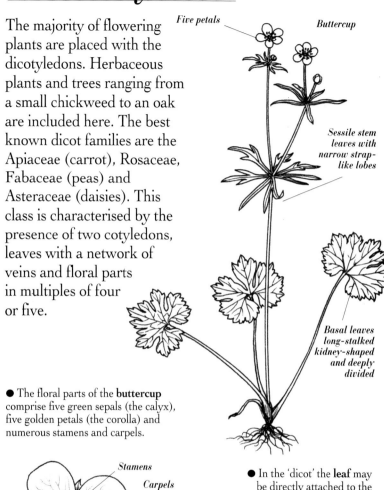

Five petals

Buttercup

Sessile stem leaves with narrow strap-like lobes

Basal leaves long-stalked kidney-shaped and deeply divided

● The floral parts of the **buttercup** comprise five green sepals (the calyx), five golden petals (the corolla) and numerous stamens and carpels.

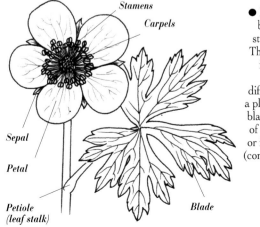

Stamens

Carpels

Sepal

Petal

Petiole (leaf stalk)

Blade

● In the 'dicot' the **leaf** may be directly attached to the stem or may have a petiole. The blade, or lamina, which is the wide flat part of the leaf, may have many different shapes. To identify a plant, you must look at this blade know if it is composed of a single part (simple leaf) or if it is divided into leaflets (compound leaf), and if these are toothed or not, and recognise the veins, etc.

Origin and History

3 thousand million years

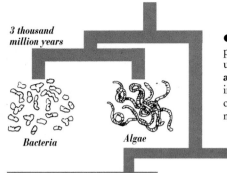

Bacteria　*Algae*

● The first plant forms able to photosynthesise were the unicellular or filamentous **blue algae**. Traces have been found in certain Precambian calcareous rocks (3000–570 million years ago).

● **Fungi** and **lichens** lack the assimilative pigments necessary for photosynthesis. Like algae, they have no stem, root or leaf.

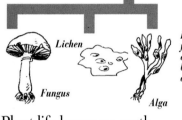

Lichen

Fungus　*Alga*

Lichens arise from an association between an alga and a fungus

Plant life began on earth with the algae three thousand million years ago. In the course of geological time, it became organised and specialised: at the present time, the flowering plants are the most numerous with more than 250,000 species.

500 million years

350 million years

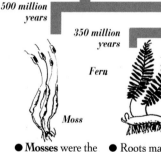

Fern

Moss

● **Mosses** were the first plants really adapted for terrestrial life.

● Roots make their first appearance with the **ferns**.

240 million years

● First **conifers** and then **flowering plants** appeared in the Mesozoic Era. From the end of the Cretaceous period onwards, the flowering plants became dominant in the plant kingdom.

65 million years

Conifer

Flowering plants

● The Middle Ages saw the rediscovery of ancient works mainly concerned with the culinary and medicinal virtues of plants.

● Medieval monks cultivated many medicinal plants in the monasteries.

● From the 16th century on, explorers brought back from their travels many plants which were to become naturalised.

● At the same time, the first herbaria and the first regional checklists were compiled.

Georges Buffon

● George Louis Leclerc Count of Buffon, the super-intendent of the royal garden (1707–1788) wrote an authoritative book *Histoire naturelle* which attempted to trace the history of animals and plants in the world.

Carolus Linnaeus

● Carolus Linnaeus (1707–1778) was the first to give plants two latin

● The 18th century was a time of learned men. The Jussieu brothers were the first to distinguish between monocots and dicots.

names, the first for genus and the second for species.

Botany

Botanists are interested mainly in wild flowers, that is, those not grown in gardens. They often begin with the most common plants beside a footpath or road and go on to rarer species hidden away in more remote places. Eventually they are led into the many aspects of ecology. After an outing, you can make a record of your trip with a drawing, a photograph or pressed flowers. Remember, it is against the law to pick flowers without permission from the owner of the land on which they grow. In fact, it is often best to leave wild flowers alone for others to enjoy.

● **Drawing** is a good way to learn about plants: you need a shrewd, keen eye for plants. But it calls for a talent which not everybody possesses.

● If you take **photographs** you can leave the plant in situ. However, you do have to get your picture in focus: make sure the plant is not blowing in the wind and that the light is right. Very good results can be obtained with a flash: if the light is reflected off a screen, a piece of white paper for example, the shadows disappear and the plant stands out clearly against a dark background.

● Some famous men were very enthusiastic botanists: for example, **Jean-Jacques Rousseau** (1715–1778) began botanising in 1765 in order to forget his political reverses. He built up a collection of pressed flowers and, more importantly, between 1772 and 1775, he wrote eight *Lettres elementaires sur la botanique* which he addressed to a four year-old girl called Madelon.

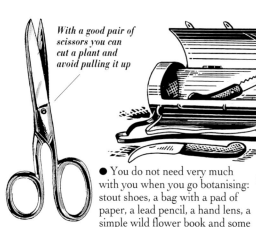

With a good pair of scissors you can cut a plant and avoid pulling it up

● You do not need very much with you when you go botanising: stout shoes, a bag with a pad of paper, a lead pencil, a hand lens, a simple wild flower book and some means of collecting plant samples (including fruit and flowers if possible).

While on site, slip the plants you have picked into envelopes

● Making a collection of pressed flowers is like filling up a photograph album.

● Slip the plants you have collected between two sheets of absorbent paper (newspaper folded in two): make a sort of protective folder and press beneath heavy books or a weight; change the paper from time to time.

● When the plant is dry, lay it out on a sheet of white paper and fix with glue at the tips only; note the latin name, date and place of collection.

Important! Before beginning a collection of pressed flowers, check which plants are protected at a regional and national level. Learn to recognise them and never pick them.

● When it is finished, the pressed material should be stored in a cupboard with naphthalene so that it does not deteriorate (insects could cause much damage). Do not forget to protect from light (which makes the colours fade), dust and humidity.

Useful or Dangerous?

In the wild, there is scarcely any plant which is not useful: some are nutritious and the wild forms have gradually been developed into cultivated forms; others are useful in fields as diverse as medicine, dyeing, perfumery, dress and even magic – St John's wort was thought to give protection against spells. But did you know that the discovery of their active principles came about gradually, through experimentation and often at the cost of human life? Testing the virtues of plants was not always without risk.

● The **wild strawberry**, found in woods and hedgerows, is a delicious fruit, **white dandelion leaves** make a refreshing salad.

● Many plants are endangered today as a result of agricultural practices which degrade their natural habitat (pesticides, drainage etc), pollution and over-collection. The law, therefore, aims to protect both the plants and the areas where they live.

● The **marigold,** a substitute for saffron, is also used in cosmetics to feed and heal the skin.

● The red petals of the **poppy** are an ingredient in cough mixtures.

● The flowers of the **cornflower,** which have anti-inflammatory properties, are used in eye baths.

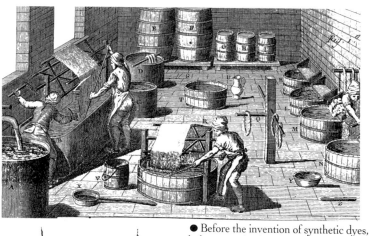

● Before the invention of synthetic dyes, clothes were dyed with natural substances mainly derived from plants.

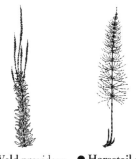

● It can be dangerous to eat certain plants, such as lords and ladies' berries or foxglove. These have active principles which are used in medicine (influencing the heart beat).

● **Weld** provides a yellow dye.

● **Horsetail** stems are used for cleaning and polishing some metals, wood and ivory. Horsetails favour damp sandy places in shade.

● In some areas, the dried fronds of **bracken** are used for animal litter.

Lords and ladies

Foxglove

Berries of lords and ladies

● **Woody nightshade** which is common in hedgerows and damp rough ground is, like meadow saffron, poisonous.

Woody nightshade

Poisonous berries

Flowers and seeds poisonous

Glossary

•ACHENE
A dry fruit containing only one seed which is not shed spontaneously when ripe.

•ACUMINATE
Describes a leaf ending in a slender point.

•ALTERNATE
Describes a leaf arising singly from a stem.

•BRACTS
Small leaves near flowers or peduncles.

•CRENATE
Edged with rounded teeth.

•EVERGREEN
Always green. Describes plants whose leaves remain green all through the winter.

•FROND
Fern 'leaf'.

•HERMAPHRODITE
Describes a flower with both stamens and carpels.

•HYBRID
Plant resulting if pollen from one species fertilises a different species.

•INFLORESCENCE
Portion of a plant bearing the flowers, a flowering shoot.

•LANCEOLATE
Shaped like a lance.

•LINEAR
Describes long very narrow leaves.

•LIP
Term used in the orchid family and some other families for the largest flower part.

•PEDICEL
Small stalk with a single flower at the tip.

•PEDUNCLE
Flower stalk, often bearing pedicels.

•PHOTOSYNTHESIS
Chemical change peculiar to plants containing chlorophyll. By using solar energy, plants are able to manufacture sugars from water and carbon dioxide and use them as food.

•RESPIRATION
The opposite phenomenon to photosynthesis, during which the plant releases enough for growth. During respiration the plant absorbs oxygen and gives off carbon dioxide.

•RHIZOME
Underground stem, often long, from which stems and roots arise.

•SESSILE
Describes a plant part (flower, leaf) with no stalk.

•SPADIX
Inflorescence on a club-like receptacle.

•SPORANGIUM
Term used for the spore-bearing structure of ferns.

•STOLON
Stem trailing along the surface of the soil and producing adventitious roots.

•UMBEL
Inflorescence in which the pedicels all arise from the same point on the peduncle.

Further Reading

Fitter R, Fitter A and Blamey M, *Collins Pocket Guide Wild Flowers of Britain and Northern Europe*, HarperCollins, London, 1996

Lippert W and Podlech D, *Collins Nature Guide Wild Flowers*, HarperCollins, London, 1994

Podlech D, *Collins Nature Guide Herbs and Healing Plants*, HarperCollins, London, 1996

Scott M *Collins Guide Scottish Wildflowers*, HarperCollins, London, 1995

Walters M, *Collins Gem Wildflowers Photoguide*, HarperCollins, London, 1994

Addresses

The Botanical Society of The British Isles
c/o Natural History Museum
Cromwell Road
London SW7 5YZ

Plantlife
c/o Natural History Museum
Cromwell Road
London SW7 5YZ

The Wild Flower Society
68 Outwoods Road
Loughborough
Leicestershire LE11 3LY

The Royal Society for Nature Conservation
The Green
Witham Park
Lincoln LN5 7JR

The Irish Biogeographical Society
c/o Natural History Museum
Kildare Street
Dublin 2
Eire

Plant Index

Flowering dates are given
in brackets.

Photographic Credits
4 P. Neveu/Colibri
5. 1 R. Toulouse/Colibri
5. 2 P. Emery/Colibri
5. 3 P. Granval/Colibri
5. 4 A. Guerrier/Colibri
6 B. Tauran/Colibri
7. 1 R. Diez/Colibri
7. 2 B. Tauran/Colibri
7. 3 C. Guihard/Colibri
7. 4 M. Bureau/Bios
23 J.-M. Brunet/Colibri
24 G. Hofer/Jacana
41 J.-L. Charmet
42 Kharbine-Tabapor

Cover illustration:
R. Mettler